Pig-Out

Pig-Out

by Christina Hanley

Citadel Press   Secaucus, N.J.

First edition
Copyright© 1983 by Christina Hanley
All rights reserved
Published by Citadel Press
A division of Lyle Stuart Inc.
120 Enterprise Ave., Secaucus, N.J. 07094
In Canada: Musson Book Company
A division of General Publishing Co. Limited
Don Mills, Ontario
Manufactured in the United States of America
ISBN 0-8065-0843-4

To My Wonderful Family: Len, Helen, Mark, Sheila
--and especially Maryellen,
whose enthusiasm and love made this book a reality

(and Tim, too, of course)

Contents

Pig-Out

No-Bake Cookies

1 stick butter
½ cup packed brown sugar
1 teaspoon grated orange rind
½ cup walnuts (chopped)

½ cup orange juice
2 cups quick-cooking oatmeal (dry)
flaked coconut

Melt butter in medium-sized pan. Add brown sugar, orange rind and orange juice, stirring until sugar is completely dissolved. Remove from heat. Stir in oatmeal and nuts. Refrigerate 1 hour, then shape into balls and roll in coconut. Makes about 42 chewy cookies. These are great as gifts during the holidays.

Pecan Pie

¼ cup butter   1½ cups pecans, broken
1 cup brown sugar   1 teaspoon vanilla or rum
3 eggs   ½ teaspoon salt
½ cup light corn syrup   1 pastry shell, partially baked

Cream the butter with the brown sugar, then beat in the eggs, one at a time. Stir in the corn syrup, pecans, vanilla and salt. Pour into the prepared pastry shell that has been only partially baked (about 5 minutes). Bake at 375° for about 40 minutes or until a knife inserted comes out clean. Serve warm or cold, but _definitely_ serve it with whipped cream.

Buttery Lemon Crisps

1 cup sweet butter, softened
1½ cups sugar
4 egg yolks
juice of 1 lemon

½ teaspoon lemon extract
2 teaspoons grated lemon rind
3 cups flour
½ teaspoon salt

Cream butter and sugar. Add the egg yolks, lemon juice, rind and extract and continue beating until light and fluffy. Mix in the flour and salt just until blended. Form into 2 long rolls, each about 2 inches in diameter (like big sausages). Wrap and refrigerate several hours or overnight. When ready to bake, preheat oven to 375°. Slice dough ⅛ inch thick and place on greased cookie sheet about 1½ inches apart. Bake 8 to 10 minutes or until light brown. Remove from pans and let cool. Makes about 7 dozen.

Mama-Mia Tortilla

butter   1 tablespoon honey

1 8-inch flour tortilla   ¼ teaspoon cinnamon

your favorite ice cream

First, butter the tortilla on both sides. Cook in a frying pan on low heat until golden brown. Place it on a plate, drizzle with the honey and sprinkle with the cinnamon. Spoon the ice cream down the middle of the tortilla, roll it up and devour promptly. This serves only one, so be sure to buy lots of everything.

Porky's Dilemma
(Divinity)

½ cup water

½ cup light corn syrup

2 cups white or brown sugar

2 egg whites

1 cup nuts, broken

1 cup raisins

First, bring the water and corn syrup to a boil in a heavy pan. Add the sugar and cook until dissolved. When boiling the mixture, cover the pan for about 3 minutes, then uncover and continue cooking for a few minutes on medium heat without stirring, to a hard-ball stage. While syrup is boiling, beat egg whites in a large bowl until they just hold their shape. When syrup is thickened, pour it gradually over the egg whites in a thin stream, whipping slowly at the same time. Toward the end, add the syrup faster and whip faster. Finally, add the nut meats and raisins. Beat until thick enough to drop onto a buttered surface to form patties that hold their shape. Makes about 1½ lbs.

Tea-Time Walnut Cake

¾ cup butter

2½ cups sugar

4 large eggs, separated

3 cups flour, sifted

2 teaspoons baking powder

1 cup milk

6 tablespoons butter, melted

1 tablespoon cinnamon

½ cup chopped walnuts

Cream butter and only 2 cups of the sugar until fluffy. Beat yolks until creamy. Fold into the butter mixture. In a separate bowl, sift flour and baking powder. Add to the butter batter alternately with the milk. Now, beat the egg whites and carefully fold into cake batter. Pour into well greased and floured tube pan. Mix the remaining ½ cup sugar with cinnamon and nuts. Sprinkle over top of cake. Spoon melted butter evenly over the top. Bake at 350° for 1 hour. Let cool a bit before removing from pan. An English delight!

Apple Dōtser Dessert

6 apples, peeled and sliced   ½ cup sugar
¼ cup raisins   20 large marshmallows

Place the apple slices in a baking dish, layer with raisins and the sugar. Repeat until everything is used up. Cover and bake at 350° for about 45 minutes or until apples are tender. Remove cover, place marshmallows on top and return to oven, uncovered, until brown. Serve with vanilla ice cream.

Lumpy's Lament

1 cup butter, softened
½ cup sugar
6 eggs
2 cups milk
2½ cups flour

4 teaspoons baking powder
1 teaspoon salt
2 tablespoons sugar
1 teaspoon vanilla
1 lb. jack cheese, crumbled

Cream the ½ cup sugar with the butter. Add 4 of the eggs, one at a time, beating well after each addition. In a separate bowl, sift the flour with the baking powder and salt. Add to the butter mixture alternately with only 1½ cups milk. Pour ½ this batter into a large, buttered casserole dish. In a blender, put the crumbled cheese, ½ cup milk, 2 tablespoons sugar, vanilla and 2 remaining eggs together. Blend until smooth. Pour this over the cake batter, spreading evenly. Top off with rest of cake batter. Bake at 325° for 1 hour. Spoon out in heaps, like a pudding. Makes enough for 8.

Swine Sweeties

2 cups flour, sifted

2 egg yolks

½ cup brown sugar

1 teaspoon vanilla

1 cup butter

1 egg white, slightly beaten

¼ cup walnuts, ground

⅛ cup jam, jelly or preserve

Mix the flour, yolks, brown sugar, vanilla and butter together until smooth. Form dough into 1-inch balls. Dip the balls into the egg white and roll in the ground walnuts. Bake on a greased cookie sheet at 325° for about 5 minutes. Remove from oven and make a dent in the center of each ball with your thumb. Return to oven and bake for 20 minutes more. When cooled, spoon a dab of jelly in each indentation. Makes about 60 cookies. These really brighten up the cookie platter and will keep 'em oinking for more.

Butter Horns

(An Aunt Jeanie Original)

1 cup butter
½ cup pecans, chopped fine
¼ cup sugar

½ teaspoon vanilla
2 cups flour

Mix all ingredients together very well. With your hands, shape about 1 teaspoon of the dough at a time into a crescent. Bake at 350° for about 15 minutes. Definitely hide some of these in the back of your freezer for a later date—they'll be gone before <u>you</u> get any!

Paiute Pudding

2 cups milk
¼ cup cornmeal
¼ cup sugar
½ teaspoon ginger
½ teaspoon cinnamon

½ teaspoon salt
⅛ teaspoon baking soda
1 cup milk
¼ cup dark molasses
whipped cream, nutmeg

In a saucepan, cook milk over low heat until hot. Add cornmeal a little at a time. Cook for 15 minutes or until it thickens, stirring constantly. Remove from heat. In a small bowl, mix together the sugar, salt, ginger, cinnamon and baking soda, then stir into the cornmeal mixture. Add the cup of milk and molasses and blend thoroughly. Pour into a 1-quart casserole and bake at 275° for about 2 hours. Serve warm with whipped cream and a sprinkle of nutmeg. Serves 6. (This wonderful recipe is credited to the Native People of this country.)

Butterscotch Pie

1 cup brown sugar
¼ cup flour
3 tablespoons butter
¼ teaspoon salt
2¼ cups milk, scalded

4 egg yolks
½ teaspoon vanilla
½ cup nut meats
whipped cream
9-inch baked pie shell

In a double-boiler, combine brown sugar, flour, butter and salt and cook until blended. Next, add the scalded milk. In a separate small bowl, beat the egg yolks until light, pour just a little of the above mixture into the yolks, mix and pour everything back into the double-boiler. Stir and cook until it thickens slightly. Beat this custard until cool, and then add the vanilla and nut meats. Pour this entire mixture into the baked pie shell. Let cool thoroughly and cover with whipped cream.

Strawberry Short Torte

9 egg whites   ¾ cups almonds, ground

1½ cups sugar   1 quart strawberries: cleaned, sliced, sugared

1 teaspoon vanilla   2 quarts heavy cream, whipped

Beat egg whites until stiff and rather dry. Gradually add the sugar, beating continuously. Add the vanilla and then fold in the nuts. Spread evenly in 2 round cake pans with removable bottoms. Bake at 325° for 25-30 minutes. When cool, put cut and sugared strawberries and whipped cream between the layers and on top. Unbelievably sinful.

Almond Butter Ribbons

1 cup sugar

½ lb. almonds, grated

1 cup butter

2 eggs

rind of 1 lemon, grated

2 cups flour

1 egg yolk

First, set aside ¼ cup sugar and nuts for final decoration. Next, cream butter with rest of sugar, eggs, rest of almonds, lemon rind and flour. Chill. Roll with rolling pin until very thin and cut into strips. Brush with egg yolk, sprinkle with the ¼ cup sugar and nuts that were set aside and bake on greased cookie sheets at 350° for 10 to 12 minutes.

Crumb Pie

9-inch baked pie-shell
½ cup raisins
1 cup brown sugar
½ hot water
3 eggs, beaten
1 cup cookie or cake crumbs

⅓ cup flour
1 teaspoon cinnamon
¼ teaspoon nutmeg
¼ teaspoon ginger
⅓ cup butter, softened

To start, sprinkle the bottom of baked pie shell with the raisins. Set aside. In a double boiler, mix together the brown sugar, hot water and eggs and cook until thick. Let cool and then pour into pie shell. Next, combine rest of ingredients and work with a fork until well mixed. Sprinkle this over the filling and bake at 325° for 20-30 minutes. (Another desperation dessert.)

Lemony Roll-Up

1 cup sugar   ¼ cup fresh lemon juice

6 eggs   sugar

2 tablespoons finely grated lemon peel

First, grease and flour a large cookie sheet. Beat the 1 cup sugar with the eggs on high speed of an electric mixer until pale yellow and rather thick. Fold in lemon juice and peel. Pour into pan, making sure to spread it evenly and to the edges. Bake in preheated 425° oven for about 13 minutes. As soon as you remove this from the oven, loosen edges with a knife. Turn it over onto a clean dish towel and dust cake generously with sugar. Very gently roll up the cake like a jelly roll. Fold towel over the rolled cake and let stand for 4 to 6 hours. Cut into ½ to ¾-inch slices and serve. Serves 6.

Chocolate Cookies

½ cup butter

1½ cups sugar

1 egg, beaten

¼ teaspoon salt

2 squares unsweetened chocolate, melted

2 teaspoons baking powder

2½ cups flour

¼ cup milk

Cream butter and sugar, then add the beaten egg, salt and chocolate. Beat well. Sift flour with baking powder and alternately add it to the butter/sugar mixture with the milk. Beat well again. Chill several hours. When ready, roll with a rolling pin until very thin and shape with cookie cutters. Bake on a greased cookie sheet at 350° for about 10 minutes.

Peanut Butter Cupcakes

½ cup butter

1½ cups brown sugar

½ cup peanut butter

1 teaspoon vanilla

2 eggs, beaten

1½ cups flour

½ teaspoon salt

2 teaspoons baking powder

⅔ cup milk

Cream butter, sugar and peanut butter. Add the vanilla and eggs, beating well. Sift together the flour, salt and baking powder. Alternately, add this to the egg mixture with the milk. Bake in greased or lined muffin pans at 350° for about 30 minutes. Frost with any chocolate frosting. Makes about 20 cupcakes. (This is a great one if you are desperate for something sweet to eat but have nothing but a bunch of miscellaneous ingredients in your cupboard.)

Peaches & Cream Dream

4 large, fresh peaches

2 cups water

¾ cup sugar

1 teaspoon vanilla

¼ teaspoon salt

2 egg yolks

¾ cup powdered sugar (sifted)

⅓ cup sherry

1 cup whipping cream

nutmeg

Peel, halve, and pit peaches. Bring sugar and water to a boil, then add peaches. Simmer for 5 to 10 minutes, or until tender. Add vanilla and chill until serving time. Beat egg yolks with salt until very thick. Add sugar slowly, and continue beating until very thick and lemon-colored. Next, add the sherry. Whip cream until stiff, and fold into egg yolk mixture. Spoon over the peaches and sprinkle with nutmeg. Grunt! Serves 6 to 8.

31

Mint Cream & Brownie Pie

3 egg whites
dash of salt
½ teaspoon vanilla
¾ cup sugar
¾ cup chocolate wafer crumbs (fine)
½ cup walnut pieces

1 cup whipping cream
sugar to taste
¼ cup peppermint stick
    candy (crushed)
1 square unsweetened
    chocolate (grated)

Beat egg whites and salt until soft peaks begin to form. Add the sugar, 1 tablespoon at a time, beating continuously until glossy. Add vanilla. Fold in wafer crumbs and nuts. Spread mixture in buttered pie pan, forming it thick along the edges. Bake at 325° for 35 minutes. Let cool. Several hours before serving time, whip cream until stiff; fold in sugar to taste and candy. Pile into pie shell. Chill. Trim with grated chocolate. Serves 6.

Minute Mousse

2 cups heavy cream, whipped
1 can chocolate syrup

Mix together. Freeze in refrigerator tray or mold. That's it!

Toffee Squares

1 cup butter

1 cup brown sugar

1 egg yolk

2 cups sifted flour

1 teaspoon vanilla

1 cup chopped nuts

6 oz. semi-sweet chocolate chips

Cream butter and sugar. Add egg yolk, flour and vanilla. Press into a greased 9x13-inch pan and bake for 15-20 minutes. Meanwhile, melt the chocolate chips. Spread on the baked dough. Sprinkle with the nuts (walnuts are best). Let cool. Makes about 30 squares.

Macaroon Magic Pie

3 squares bitter chocolate
½ cup butter
3 eggs, slightly beaten
¾ cup sugar

½ cup flour
1 teaspoon vanilla
⅔ cup sweetened condensed milk
2⅔ cups coconut (shredded)

Melt butter and chocolate in pan over low heat. Stir in sugar, eggs, flour, and vanilla. Pour into greased 9-inch pan (a pie tin is fine). Mix together milk and coconut and spoon over the chocolate mixture, leaving a 1-inch border around the rim. Bake at 350° for 30 minutes. Let cool before eating.

Bourbon Belly Busters

2 tablespoons cocoa

1 cup powdered sugar

¼ cup bourbon whiskey

2 tablespoons light corn syrup

2½ cups crushed vanilla wafers

1 cup pecans, chopped

½ cup powdered sugar

Sift together the cocoa and 1 cup powdered sugar. To that, add the whiskey and corn syrup. Mix thoroughly. Add the crushed wafers and pecans. Roll mixture into small balls. Dredge in the ½ cup powdered sugar. Eat.

"Go Bananas" Cake

2¼ cups flour
½ teaspoon baking powder
¾ teaspoon baking soda
½ teaspoon salt
1½ cups sugar

½ cup butter
2 eggs
1 cup ripe bananas, mashed
1 teaspoon vanilla
¼ cup buttermilk

Sift the flour, baking powder, baking soda and salt in a bowl. In a separate bowl, cream the butter and sugar until very light. Add the eggs, one at a time, beating continuously. In a third bowl, blend the mashed bananas with the buttermilk and vanilla. Now, alternately add the flour mixture and the banana mixture to the butter mixture. Stir well after each addition. Bake at 350° for 30 minutes in any cake pan you wish. (Be sure to grease and flour it first.)

Peanut Butter Fudgies

1 cup peanut butter   1¼ cup non-fat _dry_ milk
1 cup corn syrup   1¼ cups sifted, powdered sugar

Disgustingly simple. Mix and knead. Roll into balls. Refrigerate. Makes about 2 pounds (which changes to about 10 after digestion).

Gingerbread

½ cup butter

½ cup sugar

1 egg, beaten

2½ cups flour, sifted

1½ teaspoons baking soda

1 teaspoon cinnamon

1 teaspoon ginger

½ teaspoon salt

½ cup molasses

½ cup honey

1 cup hot water

First, melt the butter in a saucepan on low heat, then let cool. Beat together the sugar and egg and blend with the butter. In a separate bowl, sift the flour, baking soda, cinnamon, ginger and salt. In another bowl, combine the molasses, honey and hot water. Alternately add the flour mixture and the molasses mixture to the butter mixture. Stir until blended. Bake in a 9x9x12-inch pan that has been greased and floured, for about 1 hour at 350°. Scrumptious when served warm with whipped cream.

Pig-Haven Hash

about 40 mini-marshmallows   1 cup walnuts, chopped
(or 12 big ones, cut up)   1 lb. milk chocolate

To begin, line a pan with waxed paper so it's ready when you need it. Melt the chocolate in a double boiler over hot water. Pour ½ the chocolate on to waxed paper. Sprinkle the nuts and marshmallows over that, then pour the rest of the chocolate over all. Cool and break into huge chunks.

Rum-Tum-Tums

4 egg whites
1 lb. powdered sugar
½ lb. pecans, ground

½ lb. walnuts, ground
1 teaspoon vanilla or rum

Beat egg whites until stiff, then add sugar and nuts. Fold in the vanilla and/or rum and mix well. Form into rolls ¾ inch in diameter. Chill for 1 hour. Cut into ½-inch slices and bake on greased cookie sheet at 350° for about 15 minutes. While they are still warm, ice with powdered sugar moistened with enough rum to make it spreadable. These are a real delicacy.

Sour Cream Cookies

1 cup sugar

3 cups flour

1 teaspoon salt

1 teaspoon baking soda

1 teaspoon nutmeg

1 cup butter

2 eggs, beaten

1 cup sour cream

Sift the dry ingredients first. Work in the butter with a fork. Add the eggs and sour cream a little at a time, stirring all the while until well blended. Chill thoroughly. Roll out with a rolling pin and cut with your absolute favorite cookie cutter. Bake on a greased cookie sheet at 425° for about 7 minutes.

Peanut Butter Cookies

1 cup butter

1 cup sugar

1 cup brown sugar

2 eggs, well beaten

1 teaspoon vanilla

1 cup peanut butter

3 cups flour

½ teaspoon salt

1½ teaspoons baking soda

Cream butter and sugar together. Add the eggs, vanilla and peanut butter. Set aside. In a separate bowl, sift the flour with the baking soda and salt and then add it to the peanut butter mixture. Mix well and knead. Roll into balls about ¾ inch in diameter. Place about 1 inch apart on greased cookie sheets and flatten each one slightly with a fork in a criss-cross fashion. Bake at 400° for about 8 minutes, depending upon how chewy you like your cookies. (Optional: Toss in a handful or two of chocolate chips if you really want to be shameful.)

Hermits

1 cup butter
1½ cups sugar
1 cup raisins (chopped)
3 eggs

3 cups flour
1 teaspoon ground cloves
1 teaspoon nutmeg
1 teaspoon baking soda

Cream butter and sugar, add raisins and eggs, beating well. Sift the dry ingredients and add to the above mixture. Roll this out thin and cut into large-sized bars. Place on a greased cookie sheet and bake at 325° for about 15 minutes.

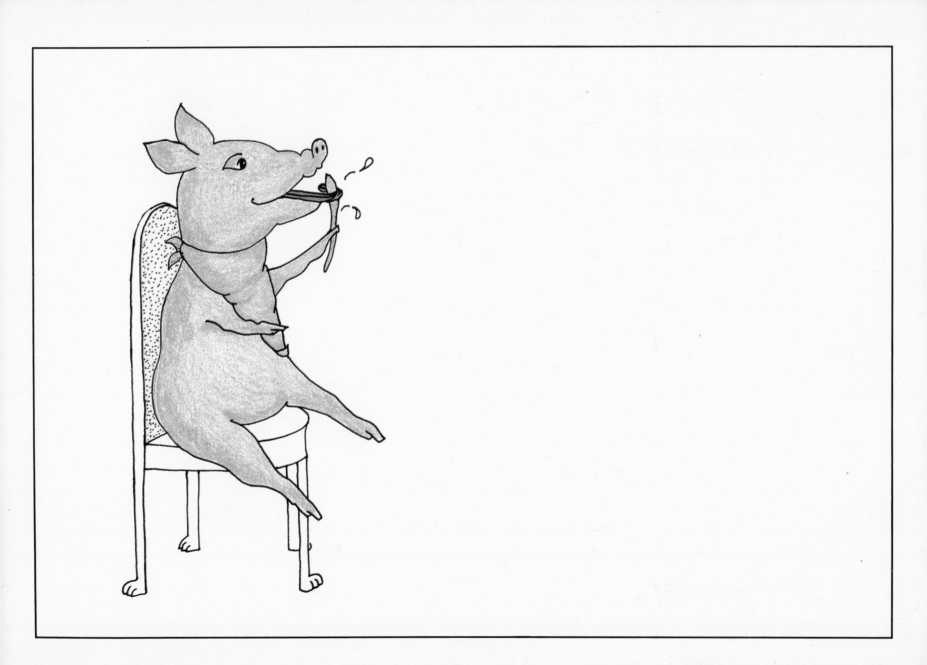

Dump Dessert

21-oz. cherry pie filling
1 tablespoon lemon juice
16-oz. can crushed pineapple
    (undrained)

18-oz. package yellow cake mix
¾ cup butter
½ cup walnuts, chopped

Dump pie filling and lemon juice into a greased 9x14-inch cake pan. Dump pineapple on top of cherry mixture. Sprinkle the dry cake mix on top of this and dot with butter. Sprinkle with nuts. Bake at 350° for 1 hour. When ready to serve, dump whipped cream on top (or ice cream). Serves about 10.

Chocolate Critters

12-oz. semi-sweet chocolate chips
2 cups raisins
2 cups salted peanuts, broken

In a double boiler, melt the chocolate chips. Let cool a bit. Add the raisins and nuts.
Drop from a teaspoon onto waxed paper and let cool thoroughly. Makes about 60
critters. (You can use chopped walnuts or pecans for this, also.)

Real Irish Shortbread

4 cups flour
2 cups butter
1 cup sugar

Mix ingredients very well until smooth. It's best to do this with your hands. Divide the dough into thirds and roll each glob into a ball. Press each ball onto a greased cookie sheet with the palm of your hand into a 5-inch disc. Jab each patty with a fork a few times. Bake at 325° for 20 minutes, making sure that they don't brown. Remove from oven. Immediately cut each into 5 pie-shaped sections. Wait until they cool completely before removing from the pan. Makes 15 large shortbreads. These are delicious dunked in coffee.

Chocolate Oinkers

4 egg whites

1 cup sugar

½ teaspoon vanilla

2 squares unsweetened chocolate, grated

6 oz. semi-sweet chocolate chips

¼ cup milk

1 cup walnuts, finely chopped

Beat egg whites until stiff. Gradually add the sugar, beating continuously. Add vanilla and grated chocolate. Mix well. Drop from a teaspoon on a greased cookie sheet and bake at 275° for 45 minutes. Remove from pan. Melt chocolate chips with milk in top of double boiler. Dip top of cooled cookies in warm chocolate and then in chopped nuts. Makes about 50 oinkers.

Pooker's Panic Cookies

1¼ cups graham cracker crumbs
⅔ cup coconut, shredded
6 oz. semi-sweet chocolate chips
14 oz. can sweetened, condensed milk

Mix everything together very well and pour into a small, square baking pan. Bake at 375° for about 25 minutes. While still hot, cut into squares and remove. Dust with powdered sugar when cool. If desired, chopped walnuts or pecans can be added instead of the coconut. Great for uninvited quests.

Cecil's Mountain

1 quart of your absolute favorite ice cream
½ cup chopped walnuts
7-inch layer sponge cake
1 cup whipping cream

2 tablespoons powdered sugar
1 teaspoon vanilla
½ cup crushed peppermint candy

Add the nuts to the softened ice cream. Pour this into a 7-inch smooth, rounded bowl and re-freeze for about 5 hours. Cut the sponge cake to form a 7-inch disc. Set this on a plate and invert the ice cream onto the cake. In a separate bowl, whip the cream, adding the sugar and vanilla. Glob this over the ice cream, spreading gently. Sprinkle with crushed candy. This is truly outrageous. Serves about 10. Excellent for late night binges.

Apricot Beauties

1 cup butter, softened

1 cup sugar

6 egg yolks

24 oz. apricot jam

6 egg whites

⅛ teaspoon salt

1 teaspoon almond extract

2½ cups flour, sifted

Topping:

1 cup sugar

1½ cups walnuts, chopped fine

Cream butter and sugar in a large bowl. Add the yolks and extract. Mix thoroughly. Add flour gradually and blend again. In an ungreased cookie sheet, press the dough firmly and evenly on the bottom. Spread with the jam. Beat egg whites slightly. Add the salt and slowly add sugar, beating continuously until stiff. Gently fold in the nuts and spread this over the jam. Bake at 350° for 45 minutes. Wait until cool to cut into squares. Makes about 70 squares.

Carrot Cake

2 teaspoons baking soda

3 eggs, beaten

2 cups sugar

1 teaspoon cinnamon

2 teaspoons vanilla

1 teaspoon salt

1¼ cups oil

2 cups flour, sifted

1½ cups shredded coconut

2 cups shredded carrots

1 cup nuts, chopped

1 cup crushed pineapple (with juice)

Mix everything together by hand until well blended. Bake in a well greased and floured 9x13-inch pan at 350° for 50 minutes. Let cool before cutting into squares. Frost with a combo of cream cheese and powdered sugar, if desired. For red-heads & rabbits only.

Coffee Fudge

1 cup strong coffee

2 cups sugar

1 tablespoon cream

1 tablespoon butter

⅛ teaspoon salt

¼ teaspoon cream of tartar

½ teaspoon almond extract
or
½ teaspoon cinnamon

1 cup broken pecans or walnuts

In a large, heavy pan bring the coffee to a boil. Remove from heat and stir in the sugar, cream, butter, salt and cream of tartar until it is all dissolved. Cook again on medium heat until it boils. Cover and cook for about 3 minutes, then uncover and cook a few minutes more. Remove from heat and let cool until just warm, not hot. Add the extract or cinnamon and beat until it begins to harden. Add the nuts. Pour into a buttered pan and let cool thoroughly before cutting into squares. Makes about 1 lb.

Peppermint Creams

2 cup sugar
¼ cup light corn syrup

¼ cup milk
¼ teaspoon cream of tartar
peppermint oil or extract

Over low heat, stir all of the above together in a heavy saucepan until sugar is dissolved. Cook until it begins to boil. Be sure to scrape the sides of the pan while it cooks. Let this cook for the last few minutes without being stirred, until it reaches a soft-ball stage. Remove from heat and let cool a bit. Beat until creamy and flavor with about 10 drops of peppermint oil or extract. At this time you can color the cream with food coloring, if you want. Drop from a teaspoon onto foil into whatever sized patties you feel the best with. Refrigerate. Great after a big dinner or at holidays.

Obscene Strawberry Cream

1 quart fresh strawberries
1 cup sugar
2 envelopes unflavored gelatin

¼ cup cold water
¼ cup boiling water
2 cups heavy cream, whipped

Set aside a handful of the berries for final decoration. Pour the sugar over the rest of the berries and let stand several hours. After they are soft and juicy, crush them. In a large bowl, put the gelatin and cold water together and stir until softened, then add the boiling water and stir until dissolved. Let cool and add the crushed berries. When mixture begins to jell, fold in the whipped cream. Chill for at least 2 hours. Decorate with the reserved berries.

You can make Raspberry Cream by simply substituting raspberries for the strawberries.

Ricotta Cheese Pie

1½ lbs. ricotta cheese   1 tablespoon flour

3 tablespoons pine nuts (toasted)   4 eggs

2 tablespoons almonds (chopped)   1 cup sugar

2 tablespoons candied citrus peel (chopped)   1¼ teaspoons vanilla

9-inch unbaked graham cracker pie crust

Mix the first 4 ingredients together until well blended. Dust it with the flour. In a separate bowl, beat the eggs until light. Gradually add the sugar and vanilla and blend well. Now add the cheese mixture to the eggs until well combined. Pour this into the pie crust and bake at 375° for about 40 minutes. Disgustingly decadent.

Blueberry Cheesecake Cookies

1¼ cups graham cracker crumbs
⅓ cup butter, melted
2 tablespoons sugar
2 8-oz. packages cream cheese

2 eggs
½ cup sugar
1 teaspoon vanilla
1 20 oz. can blueberry pie filling

Combine graham cracker crumbs, butter and the 2 tablespoons sugar in medium bowl and mix together thoroughly. Now, sprinkle 1 teaspoonful of this crumb mixture into the bottom of <u>miniature</u> muffin tins that have paper liners in them. Press the crumbs along the bottoms. Next, combine cream cheese, eggs, remaining sugar and vanilla in a large bowl. With an electric mixer, beat until well blended—about 4 minutes. Spoon 2 teaspoons of the cheese mixture into the cups. Bake until firm, about 10 minutes at 375°. Let cool. Spread 1 teaspoon pie filling on each mini-cheese cake. Keep cool until ready to eat. (You can use regular sized muffin tins, also.)

Piglet's Petits Fours

¾ cup unsalted butter
½ cup sugar
2 tablespoons whipping cream
1¼ cups sliced almonds

⅓ cup golden raisins
1 tablespoon candied cherries
1 tablespoon citrus peel (candied)
4 oz. semisweet chocolate

Prepare the pan first by lining a large, 1-inch deep cookie sheet or roasting pan with foil. Grease generously with oil. Melt butter in saucepan on low heat. Stir in sugar and blend well. Stir in cream. Add the almonds, raisins, cherries and peel and bring to a boil. Reduce heat and let simmer for about 2 minutes. Pour mixture into prepared pan, making sure to spread it evenly. Bake at 450° for about 10 minutes. Remove from oven and let cool enough so you can touch it. Turn out onto another sheet of greased tin foil. Chill thoroughly. In a double-boiler, melt the chocolate. Pour it over the candy and chill thoroughly again. Break or cut into smallish pieces. (To be eaten <u>after midnight only</u>!)

French Chocolate Mousse

2 cups milk
3 oz. sweet chocolate, grated
¼ cup sugar
4 egg yolks, beaten

¾ cup heavy cream
2 tablespoons brandy
1 teaspoon vanilla

In a saucepan, combine the milk, sugar and grated chocolate. Heat until milk is scalded on low heat. Pour a little of this mixture over the 4 beaten yolks, whip briskly, and pour it back into the chocolate mixture. Stir this continuously over low heat until it thickens. Let cool. In a separate bowl, whip the heavy cream until stiff and add the brandy and vanilla. Fold the cool custard into the whipped cream until well combined. Fill parfait glasses and chill several hours before serving. OOOO-la-la!

The Butter Bomb

4 cups flour
1 teaspoon salt
4 teaspoons baking powder
½ teaspoon mace
1½ cups butter

3 cups sugar
8 eggs
1 cup milk
2½ teaspoons vanilla
2 tablespoons brandy

To start, it's best to sift the flour before measuring the 4 cups' worth. After you measure out the 4 cups sifted flour, sift it again with the salt, baking powder and mace. In a separate bowl, cream the butter with the sugar until fluffy. Add the eggs, one at a time, beating continuously. Now, add the flour mixture alternately with the milk, vanilla and brandy. Stir only until well blended and bake at 325° for 1 hour in a well greased loaf pan. Explosively superb!

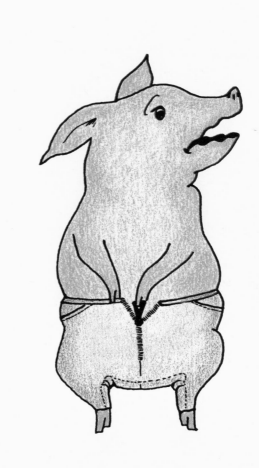

Mocha Madness Pie

2 tablespoons plain gelatin
½ cup cold water
2 tablespoons cocoa
2 cups hot, strong coffee
⅓ cup sugar
3 well beaten egg yolks

1 teaspoon vanilla
1 tablespoon brandy
1 cup whipping cream
1 tablespoon sugar
3 egg whites
9-inch baked pie crust

To start, soak the gelatin in the cold water. In a saucepan, dissolve the cocoa in the coffee and bring to a boil. Add the gelatin mixture to this and stir. Now, add the ⅓ cup sugar, mix well and let cool slightly. Next, pour this combo onto the beaten yolks and cook this in a double boiler until it thickens, stirring constantly. Let this cool until it is ready to set, and then beat with a wire whisk until fluffy. Now, add the vanilla and brandy. In a separate bowl, whip the cream with the tablespoon of sugar until stiff. In another bowl (I know this one is really messing up your kitchen, but just stick with me) whip the egg whites until stiff. _Now_, fold the whipped cream and egg whites into the coffee mixture. Pour into baked pie shell and chill thoroughly. Whew!

Hawaiian Pie

5 bananas
1 can condensed milk
½ cup lemon juice
1 9x13 graham cracker crust

1 20-oz. can crushed pineapple
whipped cream
coconut flakes

Make a graham cracker crust, press on bottom and up sides of a 9x13-inch pan. Fill bottom layer with sliced bananas. Mix lemon juice and condensed milk, pour over bananas. Spread pineapple over milk mixture. Cover with whipped cream. Sprinkle with coconut. Chill for a few hours, or overnight. Serves about 15.

World's Richest Chocolate Cake!!

¼ cup butter
¼ cup oil
2 cups sugar
1 teaspoon vanilla
¾ cup unsweetened cocoa

1¾ cups flour
¾ teaspoon baking powder
¾ teaspoon baking soda
⅛ teaspoon salt
1¾ cups milk
2 eggs

Grease and flour 2 round cake pans. Preheat oven to 350°. Cream butter, oil, sugar and vanilla until fluffy. Add eggs. Combine dry ingredients and then add that to the batter, alternately with the milk. Mix well. Add chocolate chips, if desired. Bake for about 40 minutes. Gorge!

Oatmeal Rocks

1 cup butter

1 cup sugar

2 eggs, beaten

2 cups flour

2 cups oatmeal

1 teaspoon baking powder

½ teaspoon baking soda

¼ teaspoon salt

1 teaspoon cinnamon

1 cup walnuts, chopped

1 cup raisins, chopped

¼ cup milk

Cream butter and sugar, then add eggs. Sift the dry ingredients together in a separate bowl. Now, add the walnuts, raisins, milk and butter mixture. Mix very well. Drop by teaspoonfuls on greased cookie sheets. Make sure you give them about 1 inch to move around in. Bake at 350° for about 15 minutes. These are actually good for you.

Applesauce Cake

½ cup butter

1 cup sugar

1 egg, beaten

1 teaspoon vanilla

1 cup sliced dates

1½ cups applesauce

1 cup walnuts, broken

1 cup raisins

½ teaspoon cinnamon

¼ teaspoon ground cloves

2 cups flour

2 teaspoons baking soda

Cream butter and sugar. Add the beaten egg. Toss in the remaining ingredients and blend very well. Bake in a buttered loaf pan for about 1 hour at 350°. This is a breeze—really delicious, too.

Cherry Cream Cheese Tart

1 3 oz. package cream cheese
½ cup confectioners' sugar
½ teaspoon vanilla

1 cup whipping cream
1 can cherry pie filling
     (1 lb. 5 oz.)
9-inch baked pastry shell

Cream the cream cheese, sugar, and vanilla together. Whip the cream and fold into the above. Pour into baked pastry shell, spreading evenly. Cover with pie filling. Chill before serving. Serves 6.

Lemon Coconut Cake

1 8-oz. package coconut

1 18½-oz. package lemon cake mix

1 small box <u>instant</u> lemon pudding

4 eggs

confectioners' sugar

½ cup canned coconut cream

¼ cup oil

½ cup lemon juice

¼ cup rum

First, grease a 10-inch tube pan and sprinkle bottom with half the shredded coconut. Sprinkle the rest of the coconut on a cookie sheet and broil until golden (this will take just a few seconds). Mix everything else together (except confectioners' sugar). With an electric mixer, beat at medium speed for about 3 minutes. Fold in the toasted coconut. Pour into the tube pan and bake at 350° for about 1 hour or until a knife inserted comes out clean. Let the cake cool completely before trying to remove it from the pan. After the cake is out of the pan, sprinkle with confectioners' sugar.

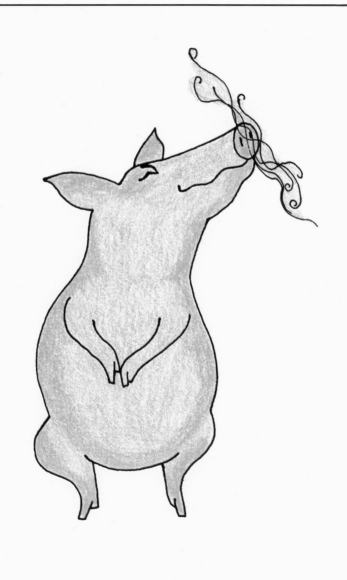

Golden Cheesecake

1½ cups graham cracker crumbs ⎫ Mix together
½ cup sugar   ⎬ and press on
½ cup butter, melted ⎭ bottom of spring pan

3 8-oz. packages creamcheese ⎫ Blend together
1½ cups sugar   ⎬ until fluffy.
1 teaspoon vanilla   ⎭ Pour into spring pan. Bake at 350° for 45 min.

4 eggs, one at a time
Meanwhile, blend:

2 cups sour cream

¼ cup sugar

1 teaspoon vanilla

Raise oven to 450° and spread sour cream mixture over cake. Bake 15 minutes longer.
Let cool 20 min. before releasing spring pan.

Bitter Chocolate Brownies

1 cup butter
1 pound unsweetened chocolate
3 cups sugar
½ cup dark corn syrup

1½ cups flour, sifted
3 teaspoons vanilla or
      almond extract
1 cup nuts, chopped

Melt the butter and chocolate together. Cool. Beat eggs, adding sugar slowly. Add cooled chocolate mixture. Blend in the corn syrup, flour, vanilla and nuts. Turn into greased and floured 8-inch square pans (2 pans). Bake in preheated 350° oven for 20-25 minutes. Makes about 48 brownies.

Butterscotch Parfait

⅔ cups brown sugar
2 tablespoons butter
⅛ teaspoon salt
½ cup water

4 egg yolks
1 cup whipping cream
2 teaspoons vanilla

Over low heat, melt the brown sugar, butter and salt in a saucepan. Bring to a boil for just 1 minute. Add the water. Cook over low heat until smooth and syrupy. Let cool. Meanwhile, beat the egg yolks. Add the cool syrup slowly, beating continuously. Cook and stir in a double boiler until fluffy. Chill. In a separate bowl, whip the cream until thick but not stiff. Add the vanilla and fold this into the chilled egg mixture. Freeze in a mold. Take out of freezer ½ hour before serving. Makes enough for 6.

Sweet Chocolate Sausage

½ lb. sweet chocolate   ½ cup almonds, sliced
1 egg   granulated sugar

Melt chocolate in double boiler, add egg. Stir until smooth and then add nuts. Spread on to a buttered surface. When completely cooled, roll into fingers 1½ inches thick. Roll in sugar, let stand until firm. Slice.

Waistline Wonders

¼ lb. sweet chocolate
½ lb. unsweetened chocolate
¼ lb. marshmallows, cut up
1 cup pecans, chopped
Confectioners sugar

Melt chocolate in double boiler. Let cool a bit, then pour over the nuts and marshmallows. Mix until marshmallows dissolve. Let cool thoroughly. When almost firm, form into balls and roll in confectioners' sugar. (I keep a bowl of these babies on my desk at all times.)

Chocolate Cream Puff Cloud

16 tiny cream puffs, 1½ inches around
½ cup light cream
6 oz. sweet chocolate
1 pint vanilla ice cream (or favorite flavor)
1 pint whipping cream

The tiny cream puffs can be made from a box mix or your own recipe. To make the chocolate sauce, pour cream in top of a double boiler. Break chocolate into chunks and add to the cream. Heat this over boiling water until melted and then beat until smooth. When ready to serve, fill each cream puff with firm ice cream. Now, drop puffs into whipped cream. Drizzle in the chocolate sauce. Blend very lightly. Heap this into a large bowl and dig in! Serves about 8.

Rocky Road Pie

12 zwiebach crackers
¼ cup butter
¼ cup sugar
¼ teaspoon cinnamon
8 small chocolate almond bars
     (⅞ oz. each)

16 marshmallows
¼ cup almonds, broken
½ cup milk
pinch of salt
1 cup whipping cream

Crush crackers into fine crumbs and mix thoroughly with butter, sugar, and cinnamon. Press into pie pan. Bake at 400° for about 10 minutes. Let cool. In top of a double boiler, melt chocolate bars, almonds, marshmallows, milk, and salt together. Let cool thoroughly. Whip cream until stiff and fold into chocolate mixture. Pour into baked pie crust. Chill until firm. (Guaranteed to inspire a jog around the block.)

Strawberry Mousse

1 quart strawberries
1⅓ cups confectioners' sugar
2 cups heavy cream, whipped

1 teaspoon vanilla
¼ teaspoon salt

Start by cleaning the berries well, if they are fresh. Add the sugar to them and let stand 1 hour. Mash and strain (but save the juice for something else you can think of). Add vanilla and salt to whipped cream. Fold into mashed strawberries. Freeze in a mold or tray of some kind, but don't stir it. You can use this same recipe with other berries and/or fruits you have mashed.

Walnut Sweet Tarts

½ cup butter
½ cup brown sugar
¾ cup white sugar
¼ teaspoon salt
¼ cup light corn syrup
4 eggs, well beaten

½ cup whipping cream
1½ cups walnuts, chopped
1 teaspoon vanilla
pastry for 10-12 small tart shells
2 cups whipping cream

Cream the butter with both brown and white sugars in a double boiler until fluffy. Stir in the salt, corn syrup, beaten eggs, and the ½ cup whipping cream. Place this over the double boiler and cook for about 5 minutes, stirring continuously. Add the vanilla and nuts. Spoon into the pastry-lined tart shells. Bake at 375° for 20 minutes. Let cool. Top with sweetened whipped cream. Makes 10-12 tarts.

Porky's Weakness

(Chocolate Fudge)

2 cups sugar (white or brown)   ½ teaspoon salt
1 cup cream   2 tablespoons butter
2 teaspoons corn syrup   1 teaspoon vanilla
2 squares unsweetened chocolate

Cook sugar, cream, corn syrup, chocolate and salt over low heat, stirring often so it doesn't burn. Boil to a soft-ball stage (235°F). Add butter and vanilla. When cooled to a warm temperature, beat until thick and creamy. Press into buttered pans. Cut into squares. (If desired, you can toss in a handful or two of walnuts, pecans, coconut or even baby marshmallows.)

Lemon Lace Pie

4 egg whites
1 teaspoon cream of tartar
1 cup sugar
½ teaspoon vanilla
coconut

4 egg yolks
juice and grated rind of 1½ lemons
½ cup sugar
1 cup heavy cream, whipped

Make meringue of first 4 ingredients. Put mixture into greased, spring form or deep pie plate. Bake at 350° for 10-15 minutes, then let cool. Filling: beat egg yolks until thick and lemon-colored. Add lemon juice, rind and ½ cup sugar. Cook in double-boiler until thick. Chill. Cover meringue with a layer of whipped cream, add lemon custard, then top it off with rest of whipped cream. Sprinkle with coconut. Chill for 24 hours. (It's well worth the wait!)

Apple Crumbly

6 medium-sized cooking apples
10-inch unbaked pie shell
1 cup sugar
1 cup graham cracker crumbs
½ cup walnuts, chopped

½ cup flour
½ cup butter
¼ teaspoon salt
½ teaspoon cinnamon
1 cup whipping cream

Peel and slice the apples, arrange in unbaked shell. Mix together the sugar, cracker crumbs, flour, nuts salt and cinnamon. Sprinkle this over the apples. Melt butter and pour evenly over the crumb topping. Bake at 350° for about 1 hour. At serving time, spoon some whipped cream on each piece. (It's best when pie is still warm.) Serves 6 to 8.

Parfait à la Pineapple

1 cup sugar
¼ cup water
6 egg yolks, well beaten

1 teaspoon almond extract
2 cups pineapple, drained
2 cups heavy cream

Add the sugar to the water in a pan and boil for 5 minutes. Pour this slowly into the beaten egg yolks. Cook over a double-boiler until mixture coats the spoon, stirring constantly. Chill, then add extract and pineapple and fold in the cream that has been whipped stiff. Freeze in a tray or mold for several hours. Serves 4-6.

Chocolate Coconut Kisses

1 square unsweetened chocolate

3 cups shredded coconut

½ teaspoon vanilla

¼ teaspoon salt

1 15-oz. can sweetened
      condensed milk

Mix everything together really well. Drop by teaspoonfuls on greased cookie sheets, 1 inch apart. Bake at 375° for 15 minutes. Remove from pans while warm. (Great to munch on between sit-ups.)

Butter Almond Squares

1 cup almonds, slivered
1¾ cups flour
1½ teaspoons baking powder
⅛ teaspoon nutmeg
½ teaspoon salt
½ cup butter
1½ cups sugar

3 eggs
½ teaspoon of:
    grated lemon peel
    vanilla
    almond extract
1 cup ground almonds

Generously butter a 9x12 inch pan. Sprinkle slivered almonds over the bottom of pan. Set aside. Sift flour, baking powder, salt and nutmeg together. In a separate bowl, cream together sugar and butter. Add eggs, one at a time, beating vigorously all the while. Add lemon peel, almond extract and vanilla. Stir until well blended. Fold in flour mixture, then ground almonds. Spoon batter over the slivered almonds in pan and spread lightly. Bake at 300° for 45 minutes or until light brown. Cut into whatever sized bars you are capable of eating. Makes about 2½ dozen normal-sized bars.

Vanilla Mousse

1 cup heavy cream
¼ cup confectioners' sugar
½ teaspoon vanilla

1 egg white, beaten stiff
¼ teaspoon salt

Whip the cream. Add to it the confectioners' sugar and vanilla. Fold in the beaten egg white to which the salt has been added. Pour into a mold and freeze without stirring. Tastes dynamite with cold fruit or hot fudge sauce over it. Serves 4.

Orange Cream Pie

½ cup sugar
¼ cup flour
⅛ teaspoon salt
1 cup milk, scalded
3 egg yolks, beaten
9-inch baked pie shell

⅔ cup orange juice
2 teaspoons orange rind,
   grated
1 teaspoon butter
½ cup pecans, chopped
whipped cream

In a double boiler, mix the sugar, flour and salt—then add the scalded milk. Cook and stir over very low heat until thick. Quickly add the beaten yolks. Beat well. Add the juice, rind and butter. Cook and stir over very low heat until it thickens slightly. Add the pecans, cool, and pour into the shell. Cover with whipped cream.